Bella Goes to the Spa

Be kind to each other

By Lucie Cote Contente

Illustrations by Majbah Uddin

©2019 Lucie Cote Contente

Bella's mother called out, "Bella are you ready to go to the spa?" "I sure am," Bella thought as she ran to her mom to have her leash put on. Bella loves car rides. Her favorite part is sticking her head out the window and having the wind blow in her face. She couldn't wait to get to the spa.

As her mom parked the car Bella thought, "Finally we're here at the spa!" I wonder which friends I will see today?" She was so excited as her mom walked her into Canine Corner Spa. Bella jumped up on the counter and said "hi" to all her friends. She noticed there was a new dog sitting alone in the corner and she looked sad.

Bella went over to the new dog and said "Hi, I'm Bella what's your name?" The dog quietly said, "My name is Luna." Bella liked Luna right away. John came over to Bella and said it was time for her bath so off they went to the bathtub.

John brought Bella to the bathtub and started giving her a bath. Bella's favorite part is when she shakes off the water and bubbles and gets John all wet. That makes her laugh.

"Time to dry you up," John said. When John turned on the blow dryer, Bella's hairs were flying everywhere. Bella knew she was going to look so pretty when he was done. As she was sitting there, Bella noticed the other dogs weren't talking or playing with Luna. She even heard Maggie, the brown poodle, make fun of Luna's hair. George, the small brown and white corgi, said Luna looked ugly. Bella was sad because she knew what they were saying was not nice!

After her hair was dry, Bella had her nails cut. She knew her spa time was almost done. She was sad about how the other dogs were treating Luna. She couldn't wait to go play with her.

Finally, Bella was done and was able to go see Luna. She didn't care what Luna looked like. Bella played with Luna and it made her so happy. It was now Luna's turn for a haircut. Bella sat near her and they talked while Molly brushed Luna's fur. The other dogs couldn't understand why Bella wanted to be Luna's friend because she hadn't had a haircut in a whole year!

The more Bella talked to Luna the happier Luna felt. The other dogs noticed the more the groomer cut Luna's hair, the prettier she was getting. Eventually the other dogs started talking to Luna, too. Bella and Luna smiled because they were so happy that everyone had become friends. Molly put a pink kerchief around Luna's neck and felt so pretty.

Before Bella left the spa, John put a pretty purple kerchief around her neck. Bella had such a fun time at the spa today. She met a new friend named Luna and she saw all her other friends.

As Bella walked out of Canine Corner Spa, she was happy knowing that all the dogs would be nicer next time they met a new dog at the spa, no matter how they looked. Bella walked out the door barking "Bye everyone, see you next time!" As she walked to the car she thought "Spa day is the best!"

On the way home Bella's mom told her how proud she was of her for making friends with Luna even though the other dogs didn't want to. The dogs learned an important lesson at the spa today that Bella already knew. Just because someone doesn't look like you, doesn't mean they aren't nice. Let's just be kind to each other.

Lucie Cote Contente has also published:

Bella From the Farm

Gluten and Gluten Free Cooking in Perfect Harmony

Gluten and Gluten Free Cooking in Perfect Harmony Take 2

Gluten and Gluten Free Cooking in Perfect Harmony Take 3

Visit the website

www.luciecotecontentebooks.com

Grandma loves you JJ and Alex

www.ingramcontent.com/pod-product-compliance
Lightning Source LLC
Chambersburg PA
CBHW040244100426
42811CB00011B/1148